D1307402

# CITY WITHOUT PEOPLE

*The Katrina Poems*

# WORKS BY NIYI OSUNDARE

## Poetry

*Random Blues*
*Days*
*Tender Moments: Love Poems*
*Early Birds: Poems for Junior Secondary, Books One to Three*
*The Word Is An Egg*
*Horses of Memory*
*Seize the Day*
*Midlife*
*Waiting Laughters*
*Songs of the Season*
*Moonsongs*
*The Eye of the Earth*
*A Nib in the Pond*
*Village Voices*
*Songs of the Marketplace*

## Selected Poems

*Pages from the Book of the Sun: New & Selected Poems (1983–2001)*
*Selected Poems (1983–1991)*

## Drama

*Two Plays*
*The State Visit*

## Essay

*Thread in the Loom: Essays on African Literature and Culture*

## Public Discourse

*Dialogue with My Country*

# CITY
# WITHOUT
# PEOPLE

*The Katrina Poems*

**by Niyi Osundare**

Interview: Antoine, Rebeca, "New Orleans is People," from *Voices Rising II: More Stories from the Katrina Narrative Project.* UNO Press, 2010, 363–380. Reprinted courtesy of UNO Press, © 2010.

Black Widow Press is an imprint of Commonwealth Books, Inc., Boston, MA. Distributed to the trade by NBN (National Book Network) throughout North America, Canada, and the U.K. All Black Widow Press books are printed on acid-free paper, and glued into bindings. Black Widow Press and its logo are registered trademarks of Commonwealth Books, Inc.

Joseph S. Phillips and Susan J. Wood, Ph.D, Publishers
www.blackwidowpress.com

Cover Design: Kerrie Kemperman
Typesetting: Kerrie Kemperman
Front Cover: FEMA image provided by IP
Back Cover: USAF image provided by IP

ISBN-13: 978-0-9837079-1-2

Printed in the United States

10 9 8 7 6 5 4 3 2 1

For Kemi,

in memory of those
endless hours in the attic,


and lots more...

# Contents

## III. THE LANGUAGE OF PAIN

## IV. KATRINA WILL NOT HAVE THE LAST WORD

## V. AFTERWORD

## INTERVIEW

# PREFACE

*Beyond the Invisibility of Pain*

It is five years now since Hurricane Katrina swept through the Gulf Coast with a near-apocalyptic ferocity, inflicting sundry losses and countless bereavements. The catastrophe wrought by this storm changed many lives for ever: the child who lost an only parent; the painter who lost his favourite work; the pianist who lost a piano passed down from many generations; the professor who lost her library; the writer who lost his manuscripts; the businessman who lost his factory; the singer who lost her voice (literally and figuratively); a city which (nearly) lost its niche; a people who lost their dignity...

The intervening years seem to have erased the immensity of this catastrophe as public interest appears to have receded with the flood. The common belief now is that New Orleans has been rebuilt or is being rebuilt at a fast and even pace—a partial myth that is a reflection of the partiality in the recovery pattern of the city itself. For while the business districts have sprung back to power and tourism is back on the bloom, while neighbourhoods belonging to the rich and well-connected have bounced back with their well laundered lawns and glittering fences, those parts owned and/or inhabited by most Black and poor people are still in a state of shocking blight and neglect...

Katrina's wounds run deep; its pains are still red and stubbornly raw. As one of those gruesomely afflicted by its devastation, I remember what it meant to stand in front of my class in January 2006, a professor without books, a writer whose manuscripts and professional documents had been washed away, a 'Katrina returnee' without a place to lay his head. I waited in vain for a genuine institutional interest in and concern about the specific depth and range of my loss/pain, for a demonstration of empathy and care beyond political platitudes, official bulletins, and media sound bites which only ended up as a mockery of my pain. None came. Alas, in the mass grave to which the city's woes had been consigned, there was hardly any room for a consideration of the agonizing specificity of individual loss. Back in New Orleans, I became, to borrow the words of the Nigerian poet Christopher Okigbo, 'the sole witness of my homecoming'; the invisible carrier of my own cross... The relentless, excruciating pain of the disaster appears to have been privatised and driven into the domain of personal angst, accorded political mention only during media-hyped anniversaries and commemorations...

But who is there to listen to the deep, personal cry of the sorely afflicted, the chilling fears and anxieties of someone suddenly confronted with a future without a purpose, the silence of those whose dreams have transmogrified into nightmares? Who has the eye to see the colour of pain?

Here, again, face to face with the anonymity of loss, the invisibility of pain. The bereaved, the dispossessed, the terribly traumatized have been largely left to lick their wounds; urged to pull up themselves by their boot straps (even when those boots have been taken away by the ravaging flood); inveigled into accepting responsibility for a catastrophe that was not their own making. We have been asked to get all up and move on. Does anyone care about the relative state of our legs?...

The poems in this volume have been long in coming. (Deep tragedy hardly lends itself to instant messaging). If they do not come across as *pretty* to some readers, it is because the events which provoked them are far from pretty. Indeed, Katrina's devastations are the type that cut straight to the bone, necessitating a testimony that transcends trivial versification and verbal placebos. These poems insist on breaking the silence precipitated by the combined forces of anonymity and invisibility which often stand between the needy cry and the listening world. These are the words of someone right in the eye of the storm, *written by himself*, not 'gathered' by an unappointed spokesperson or ventriloquised from 'reliable sources' by a privileged and distant secondary source. For, although Katrina may have taken all I had away, it never succeeded in taking away my tongue—and sense of proportion and justice. It has never taken away the necessity for the telling of a truth that never rests until it has been told...

In many ways, the poems in this book are a kind of 'thank you song' for the hundreds of people here in the United States and other parts of the world who reached out to me and my family with inspiring love, generosity, and compassion. They brought a new, urgent resonance and poignancy to that famous Yoruba saying, *Enia lasoo mi* (People are my clothes). It was they, indeed, who made sure that Katrina never had the last word.

These poems are also a tribute to New Orleans, our city: its fertile energy, its irrepressible vitality, its rainbow vernacular, its music and magic, the unsinkable humanity in the core of its being. Yes, New Orleans is still there, busy getting fat every *Mardi Gras,* and penitently lean the day after. The Mississippi flows on in its muddy majesty, even as the pelican jazzes up the sky with the riff and rhyme of its glide. I sing of a city which insists on its own right to *life, liberty, and the pursuit of happiness,* earnestly hoping that the levees will one day be as strong as they ought to be, the floodwalls as enduring; a city restored to glory through equitable recovery and lasting justice.

Niyi Osundare
Aug. 29 – Sept 7, 2010

10

# I.

# WATER,    WATER !...

# THE LAKE CAME TO MY HOUSE

It all began as a whisper among
The leaves. The tree's tangled tale
And the wanton narrative of the wind

Then, the pit pat pit pat bing bang bing
Of the hooves of the trampling rain
My shuddering roof, my wounded house

A shunting of shingles
Unraveling of rafters
And the wind dropped a pool

In my living room. The sky
Rumbled like a stricken bull;
Lightning zigzagged its fire through

The darkening clouds. Wind-driven,
Tornado-tormented, the Lake overran
Its fence, pouring its piled-up anger

In the careless streets.
Levees (built with levity)
Collapsed like hapless mounds

   Roads lost their names,
   Streets their memories

A torrential torment enthralled the city
The day the Lake came down my street
And took my house away.

## KATRINA ANTHEM

Ka ka Katrina, shameless witch
Who quenched our lights and swamped the switch
Atop your stick and stormy broom
You spread your rot from room to room

Swollen with filth and fecal froth
Billowing like a bully back and forth
Heavy with stench and rancid smell
The streets decay from your toxic spell

Mistress of mess and blind campaign
Author of the plague and total pain
You dissolve the roads in your smudgy slime
And cut our day in its sunny prime

Blood on your hand, skulls in your fridge
You swamp the river and swallow the bridge
In your crowded kitchen a foul fleshfeast
Fit for the monster and the hellish beast

On the marble wall the brown scum lines
And your deadly route that twists and twines
Your mud everywhere on the tallest roof
For your killing fury the clearest proof

Tossed on your flood a gentle toy
That yesterday was some baby's joy
To the lonesome widow what a pain you bring
In your murky water her wedding ring

A whole city sprawls in your fatal grip
From its severed loins to its broken rib
A place once astir with a joyous crowd
Is now supine beneath your shroud.

## LIQUID CITY

Liquid nights
Stony skies

Angry winds whip
Treetops with the fury

Of their branches
Famous boulevards

Dissolve into nameless pools
Houses roam the streets

In search of missing roofs
The city we knew

Went away with the storm
Without leaving a forwarding address

## OMIYALE*

The Lake came to my house
(Absolutely uninvited),
Its wild waters pounding the porch

Like a band of wailing monsters
It barged through the door without knocking
Tore through the windows like a desperate burglar

Swelled up the carpet, billowed up the walls
Daubed my paintings in its own satanic colours
Sat briefly on my sofa, its dirty legs

On the coffee table, capsized my happy mugs,
Tossed up the tv like a Disney toy
Then lunged towards my crowded kitchen

My drunken fridge popped open
A frozen tilapia floated languidly
Before vanishing into the watery depth;

Swiftly followed by acres of rice
And oceans of rare spices
My *habanero* puree ignited no fire

In the mouth of the foraging felon
Which swallowed the stove
And micro-waved the oven

Down in my study
It reduced all the books
To their old, illiterate pulp

Dyed my wardrobe in
Its monochromatic mess.
And hit the street in my favourite garment

A fellow more greedy, I never saw
Until the day the Lake came to my house
Absolutely uninvited


*Literally, Water-called-at-the-homestead: a Yoruba name for home-
  devastating floods.

# SODDENLY

All so sodden
The ground under my feet

The carpet's saturated sneer
The stench and stain

Of bloated sofas
There is a soggy sadness

In the corner
Where a flower-pot

Once roared, green,
Towards the ceiling

A squeaking squelch
Surprised my sole

In the deadening air
Of the living room

Where laughter once rumbled
Like thunder from a friendly sky

All water
All waste

All drenched dreams
And constipated truths

When the Lake came
To my house

It left behind no dry eye
Or mudless foot

## WATER NEVER FORGETS

Water has its own memory,
its drip-drop, drop-dead
hints, its mindscape of echoes

So when we steal its swamps
un-fin its fishes
and trample its shells

When we scoop its heart
steel its span
and cement its stomach

It never fails
to roar back and reclaim
its trespassed honour

Water has memory
its mouth sizzles
with vengeful teeth

# PATH OF THUNDER

Same old route
Same old wind

From Africa
West and wild

Enraged by the sun
Inspired by the season

Through hemorrhaged islands
To the eastern flanks of the leviathan West

Howling through canefields
And cotton-bales white with Negro sweat

A boiling ocean unleashes its fury
It bottom heavy with nameless bones...

So many tales yet untold
Inhabit the lips of these unruly winds

## PEDIGREE

Tyrone's grand father
heard Betsy's echoes
in Katrina's howl

His mother discerned
the killsome cornea of Andrew
in the new storm's eye

So many horses of pain
have galloped through these shores
each with its own aftermath

Of blood and tears
but none has left hoofprints
as deep and wide as Katrina's scars

## TELL ME, RAIN

Tell me, Rain
Tell me, Rain

Tell me now
Before the Thunder-god arrives

Are you a whiff of sound
In the ear of the sky

Or one brave tear
From the eye of the sea

You strike the road
It runs red with mud

You hit my bread
It swells like a sickly mound

You touch the pool
It becomes a lake

You intoxicate the lake
It bursts its banks

You rattle my roof
And hurt my house

My books dissolved
In your thieving floods

"Stay in your sky!",
I almost exclaimed

Then I remembered
Thinning rivers

And burnt-out lawns
The dormant seeds

In the belly of the earth
Silent hints of coming harvests.

## THE RAIN HAS A STORY

This year's rain
Has a story

    as viscous as its waters
      fetid as its freight of ruined fortunes

This year's rain
Has a song

    sour like its whistling winds
      sad like its funerals

This year's rain
    muddied a city's magic
      stole the people's name

This year's rain
    danced on the grave
      of many dreams

# DEATH CAME CALLING

Death came calling
It never met me at home

It met *aruwele*,[1] shrub of the moon
Dancing dreams and waving ferns
And the crab's small eyes and sleepless gaze
The timeless smile on the face of the sun

It met a clump, dusty-red
Stubbed its toe on the Rock of Life
Fell face down like a footless foe
Lost its teeth and clipped its claws

It met Olosunta,[2] Father of Rocks
It met Oroole[2] Ruler of Lofty Heights
It met Esidale,[3] Founder of Earth and Sky
It met Ifa,[4] Source and Living Wisdom

It met me shielded
By a cloak of kindness
The quenchless fire of the human soul
Hope whose flair defies the flood

Death came calling
But it never met me at home.

---

[1] Aruwele: new shrubbery that comes with the first rains.
[2] Olosunta and Oroole are two of the most prominent rockhills in Ikere, birthplace of the poet. Also worshipped as deities.
[3] Esidale is the spirit of Earth, of Origins.
[4] Ifa is the Yoruba god/medium of wisdom, divination, science, poetry, and philosophy.

# EMERGENCY CALL

911   911
Water from the Lake
Is just below my porch

*Oh, make it stop dead*
*In its tracks*

911   911
Water from the Lake
Is right at my door

*Oh, command the door*
*Not to open a bit*

911   911
Water from the Lake
Is coming through the window

*Oh, pull down the shutters*
*Unwind the blinds*

911   911
The roof is rent
The ceiling is falling

*Oh, look at the stars*
*The sky is comfort zone*

911   911
There is nine feet of water
In my living room

*Oh, unfurl your fins*
*And swim like sharks*

911   911
We're trapped in the attic
And the water is rising

*Oh, get on your roof*
*For the copter men*

911   911
But it's two o'clock at night
And it's dark as hell

*Oh, pray to the holy Angels*
*They'll send you wings and a chariot of fire.*


911   911

*Pooooh poooh poooh*
*Silence…*

# II.

# AFTER THE FLOOD

# ANNIVERSARY

*(And the celebrants filed in,*
*each bearing a red rose)*

| | |
|---|---|
| A | rose |
| for | each |
| person | cat |
| or | dog |
| killed | or |
| maimed | by |
| Katrina's | storm… |
| The | thorns |
| for | our |
| tears | the |
| petals | for |
| our | Hope |
| the | stalk |
| for | our |
| strength | the |
| fragrance | for |
| our | Faith. |
| The | red |
| red | hue |
| for | the |
| river | in |
| our | veins |

*At the University of New Orleans (UNO's) first Katrina anniversary, Aug. 29, 2006.

# THIS TIME LAST YEAR

*(Katrina's 1st Anniversary)*

This time last year
Monster winds usurped the sky
The Lake rose and swallowed the streets
Alligators danced in our living rooms

This time last year
The city's roads lost their way
In the grand dissolution of civic order
Bridges groaned beneath the floods

This time last year
A massive mess invaded our homes
Pesticides sizzled into humancides
Sewage pipes emptied their bowels in the waters

This time last year
Harried from our hearth
Expelled from our homes
We littered rooftops like motley rags

This time last year
Feeble from fear, wasted by want
We dropped like hapless fruits
Into the ravenous torrent

This time last year
The multitudes asked for bread
And got a loaf of rock
And government was on leave

This time last year
Anarchy ruled the streets
Civil order dissolved in the rains
Gunshots unnerved the air

This time last year
Corpses floated freely along the lanes
Mothers mourned their missing children
Husbands lost track of their stranded wives

This time last year
Our joy stubbed a toe
Laughter took (temporary) leave
Of our parting lips

\*          \*          \*

All because the levees broke
At the faintest hint of Katrina's stroke
The footless wall that government built
Collapsed apace with the foulest guilt

They sent men and women to the farthest moon
For elusive gift and fairy boon
All over the globe their troops are found
But here at home our woes abound

All too loud the political noise
From the people of power and their pose and poise
They bellow fake promise from the rooftop high
Then vamoose without a sigh

We count the hours in the jaws of the flood
Fire in our eyes, in our anxious blood
What a way to die in a plague foretold
The strong, the weak, and the very old

We're the messy mass, the forgotten tribe
Butt of the sharp and wicked jibe
In the land of the brave, home of the free
We dangle freely from the top of the tree


\*      \*      \*


This time last year
The flood took our city away
But, somehow, Hope
Kept its head above the waters


This poem was first performed on Katrina's first anniversary at the Goldmine, French Quarter, New Orleans, August 2006.

# CITY WITHOUT PEOPLE

The trees are dead
The birds are gone

The grass is scorched
The worms have vanished

Skeletal houses stare at the sky
Through their broken windows

The streets are a running
Golgotha of rot and rubble

Masked undertakers pound the pavements
Bemoaning a shortage of coffins

One rotten trick away from speculators
In fancy phrases and mafia goggles

Lost lanes
Bombarded boulevards

In the twilight sky
A vanguard of vultures

Tell me

What do you call a house
Without walls?

What do you call a city
Without people?

This careless consequence
Of a disaster foretold

## THE CITY

is
8 feet
below sea level

The people
are
many, many miles
below government care

# POSTMORTEM

## I

Lakeisha's grandma
Drowned here
In her wheelchair
When the water rose
Above her head

A Good Samaritan
tethered her floating body
to an electric pole
to prevent it from

Getting washed away
by the raging flood

## II

Narita's baby
died in this house

The Lake stole him
from his cot

And gave him
to the hungry sea

## III

Sniffer-dogs
Have just unearthed another body:

A six-year old girl
(or thereabout)
with her bones neatly packed

in her denim pinafore,
her plastic toy
one muddy inch

from her contorted fingers.
She left no clue
About Mommy's whereabouts

## IV

Another skull
just discovered

In House 10
Road 7

Negroid
aged about 70

Probably loved fried chicken
black-eye beans and collard greens

Judging by
the shape of the teeth

We leave the Coroner's Office
to put a name to the bones

## V

A pair of boots
stands at attention

Atop the grave
Of a rubbled home,

bloated by the flood,
its medaled memory muddied

And bravely sad.
Once saw action

In Normandy
trudged through purple paddies

In Saigon
Everywhere in search

of a prize
which eluded him at home...

A sad, vacant pair
still in search of their missing feet

## VI

The Sheraton
towers above the muddy mess

Its own wound
bandaged with brown paper

Once thought impregnable
until Katrina turned its rooms

Into a rubble of broken glass

## VII

So much there was here
So little now
But

Hope, thin-bodied,
Is bent
Never broken

# ACT OF GOD

Serves them right:
Those bawdy dwellers
Of Sin City

Big Sleazy
Prancing peccadilloes
Days dark with misdeeds

Nights aglow with blood.
And their craven idols
And painted masks

Emptied bottles and crowded clubs
And staggering shadows
And flashing boobs

And wiggling waists.
The damnable excess
Of their Fat Tuesday

Their sinful Saints
And wingless Angels
The boom boom burst

Of Bourbon Street
Those revels and revelers
Their feet far too broad

For the straight 'n narrow way
And their drums, their drums
Their devil, devilish drums…

The mamby pamby
Mumbo jumbo
Of their voodoo hoodoo…

All hail Katrina,
The ultimate Avenging Angel!

## KATRINA'S DIASPORA

*(known to the Press as "Katrina Refugees")*

Dad was bused off to Albuquerque

Mon found herself in Utah

First daughter was Black-Hawked to Ashtabula

Second son hitch-hiked to Wala Wala

Back to the auction lock
Again

A new diaspora
Of desperate dislocations
And placeless destinations

Homeless again,
In Babylon.

# LOWER 9TH WARD

The higher the water rose
The lower dipped their hope

Some sought succour
In the hammock of prayers

Some swung from treetops, legs
Dangling like those of broken puppets

They called 911
Till the lines went dead

And the City's tongue
Drowned in its mouth

Many simply dropped
Like fruits unripe

Into the borderless jaws
Of the raging floods

Their names unknown
Their skeletons unfound

Supremely invisible
Even in the 'after-life'

# THE FINAL SOLUTION

He was snatched
From the jaws of the flood

By a Good-Samaritan neighbour
And bussed off to a place beyond the map

One month and two weeks later
He was back

To find all he owned
Had gone with the wind

He looked up at the sky
The sun had danced beyond his gaze

The ground beneath his sole
Was an abyss of no return

\*

*He did it the clean way:*
*No flashing knife*
*No screaming gun*
*He simply went to bed one day*
*Refusing to stir the next*

*The Coroner's Office is still*
*Wondering what file to put his case*

# CENSUS

Here on the cheap
In this monster heap

The city's wasted wealth
Sprawls in piles of death

Vital secrets of inner rooms
Side by side with toilet brooms

Grandma's wedding ring
Lies somewhere here, a vanished thing

The photo of Uncle John at eight
Decays under this unsightly weight

Ann's toy, Mama's favourite comb
Lost in a vast and nameless tomb

Sullied paintings, bloated books
Priceless garments far from their hooks

This motley mess, this unspeakable loss
Wordless prayers, unbearable cross

Mammoth mountain, desperate crowd
Who will count the corpses beneath this shroud

# THE MISSING ALTAR

God lived here
Before the flood
With his angels and archangels

But the wind unroofed the altar
Raging waters pushed the walls
Three blocks from their sacred site

Now, bloated bibles peruse the blight
The flock is off to greener pastures
Alien hymns harass the wind

## FLYING SAUCER

The roof of Tyrone's ancestral home
Was swept off the walls

Flew fifty yards down the block
Before landing on top of

Three cars flipped upside down
Like beached whales

# DISASTOURISM

Careful now,
Dear Tourist

Mind the bristling bones
Beneath your sole

Metal objects about,
Sharpened by the blunt blindness

Of a nonchalant government;
Mind those trampled tales

And muffled dreams
Which rose, declined and fell

Like ghetto empires
Of the seething South...

Careful now:
Strange voices in the air

Unsling your camera
Unleash your lenses

# THE WRECKER'S BALL

*At the intersection of Paris and Mirabeau, a poster proclaims:*

## WE TEAR DOWN HOUSES FOR A LIVING*

The wrecker's ball
is swinging in our street

swing swing swing
it's swinging in our street

unraveling the roofs
pummeling the walls

swing swing swing
it's swinging in our street

eerie chorus of broken glass
Golgotha of mangled metal

swing swing swing
it's swinging in the street

the road has vanished
beneath a riot of rubble

swing swing swing
it's swinging in our street

all all around
the smell of dust and death

swing swing swing
it's swinging in our street

the steam shovel's mouth
is crammed with buried treasures

swing swing swing
it's swinging in our street

<hr />

\* Advertisement of one of the numerous demolition companies that
swooped down on New Orleans in the wake of Katrina.

## LONDON AVENUE CANAL
*(whose levee broke and let out the Lake)*


*Gbaga gbogo gbaga*
*Gbigi gbaga gbigi*

Giant cranes
roar into the clouds
steam shovels frighten the terrain
with their glittering teeth

All around
a battery of humming leviathans
helmeted experts
and wizards from the drawing board

Everywhere
a quarry of clay
mountains of sand
and steel pylons

Patching that hole
in the levee which leaked the Lake
that drowned our homes
and buried our bones/joy

SLOW
      MEN
            AT
                WORK

How so bravely
they strive to secure the gate
after the horse's tragic escape

*Gbaga gbogo gbaga*
*Gbigi gbaga gbigi*

# FORGOTTEN

Forgotten now

The levees which broke
and emptied the Lake into the city

Forgotten:

Those who built storm walls
with dirt and rusted steel

Forgotten:

The agony of hordes without homes
hands without fingers

Forgotten:

Corpses rotting at the water's edge
Babies with missing mothers

Forgotten:

The politician's perfidy
the callous calculations of ballot-baiters

Forgotten:

Fallen oaks and bilious bayous
pelicans with broken songs

Forgotten:

The city which gave the country its past

# AFTER THE FLOOD

The world I see now
Seems to wear a different colour

The trees are taller
With a greener tinge

The sun seems to rise
From a different sky

Rivers lisp their lyrics
In a strange and strident way

There is an added tenor
To the music of the wind

The road confronts my sole
With a litany of questions:

How much can you own
How much can you disown?

How can you possess
Without being possessed?

The flood has come and gone
But it left its silt behind.

# III.

# THE LANGUAGE OF PAIN

## THE LANGUAGE OF PAIN

There is something universal
About the language of pain

The accent of jarring nerves
Desperate spasms in the muscle of the soul

Nights full of fright
Days dazzled by the sun

In the swollen joint of heavy hours
Seconds drag their broken tendons

An arthritic cacophony musics the maze
Of knuckles done bare by ceaseless knocking

There is something universal
About the language of pain

Martyred moments
Hidden tears of open wounds

The longitude of loss plays vital
Games with the latitude of laughter

# THE WEEPING BOOK

There is a weeping book in my flooded room
On a swollen carpet and disheveled broom
Its voice is muffled, its spine is broken
For weeks and weeks it has never spoken

A prattling prince once, and very smart
With gems of wisdom from every part
It sparkled with science and golden words
That sang and surged like magic birds

My constant consort, my fairest friend
Beyond every fad and fickle trend
It stood sane, secure on my crowded shelf
A lively boost to my seeking self

Then came Katrina and its frantic flood
And its gang of mess and mush and mud
Its sweeping plague and rampant rampage
Undid my treasure from page to page

A maddening mold has eaten the leaves
Which drop down dead in bales and sheaves?
A sickening swamp in my house of mirth
The tomes are robbed of their lively girth

Gone are the pages with their dainty dots
My scrawled remarks and random thoughts
My ceaseless quarrel with friendly foes
Now submerged in Katrina woes

A dreadful absence, a mournful miss
A grave bereavement it surely is
A whole life's labour is washed away
By the murderous madness of Katrina's sway

# MARES OF NIGHT

*(Sept. 16, 2005; first day at Rocky Road House, Rindge, NH)*

Always, they come at night
When darkness walks the streets
And houses wear their eaves
Like leaden shrouds

In the thin space
Between my restless eyes
I behold their train
Of skeletal sighs

And disembodied whispers.
Floating me-wards
My favourite pamphlets
From the muddy depths

Broken spines of treasured tomes
Effigies of remembered texts
Bounteously bound
Now bloated like abandoned corpses

Pages which once smiled
At my probing eyes
Glued shut by dull, illiterate mold
Metaphors dance limbless

In the watery fray
Sentences stagger in the brew
Loose-jointed, severely skewed...
They come, always, at night

When the stars are too dim
To count their beads
And the dew drops like hail
On my memory's roof

The mares gallop at night
Laden with bloated losses.

# LOSSES (1)

Dreams born
Dreams un-born

Finished songs resting
Neat in vanilla folders

Unfinished cogitations
Rippling in 'Pending' files

On desks pock-marked
With pregnant doodling

Metaphors on the make
Similes waiting for felicitous pairing

Hyperboles swollen
With pompous laughter

Well-wrought oxymorons
Dry-eyed in the watery

Inferno in my study...
Long used to the lyrical lilt of the Lake

My ears rose against the sudden
Cacophony of ugly water

The dispossessing fury
Of its marauding passion

## LOSSES (2)

*(Or laundry-list from a dirty flood)*


My half-formed song
My favourite book

A new pair of shoes
Received on Fathers Day

An African attire
Embroidered in timeless silk

A papyrus scroll
From my last Egyptian journey

A hand-made copy
Of my book in Czech

My daughter's diploma
My wife's resume

A rare, rare photo
Of my father in his youth

Tapes of a chat
With my ageing mother

My faithful fridge
My talking box

My long-owned bag
And their intimate secrets

My priceless painting
My music pack

My brainy computer
And its wondrous ways

A long-kept letter
From a childhood friend

A brand-new sofa
That indulged my snooze

A space-age mattress
For my grouching back

My long-held illusion
About caring governments

My trust in levees
Made of dirt

My boundless laughter
And care-free capers

# WITH THE NIB OF A BORROWED PEN

I eke out the season's songs
With the nib of a borrowed pen
Mine lies buried in the fetid
Waters of a wasted city

Rainbow papers, soft & slippery,
Rot in the monochromatic mess
Of care-less mud, their lines
Obliterated in the toxic cocktail

Of a wild, illiterate swamp.
When the Lake came to my house
It chewed my shelves and swallowed my books
Snapped my pen like a hapless twig

The file cabinet reluctantly
Divulged its ministry of secrets
Index cards collided with sketchbooks
In their desperate dive for muddy depths

Jotted hints, scribbled hunches
Doodled dreams, chapterless musings
In the epic of a city fore-warned
But tragically un-fore-armed.

# INSIGHT

Sometimes we never know
The import of life
Until we have touched
The threshold of death

Sometimes we need
The cruel pangs of hunger
To appreciate the kind
Generosity of food

Night plays up
The possibilities of day
Mean adversaries the value
Of genuine friends

I look up at the sky
And I see the sea
I ask for a bowl of sand
And I get a bevy of beads

The snake may sometimes
Look like an earthworm
Life is hardly ever
What it seems to be.

# LESSON

How gingerly Katrina re-
Arranged my needs

Cleared my cluttered wardrobe
Decongested my shelves

Separated me
From my bank accounts

Told me a thing or two about
The tyranny of things

Katrina showed me

The vanity of possessing,
The horror of being possessed

# KATRINA TAUGHT ME

How

to live with nothing

to tease the breeze and forgive the wind

to treasure every moment as if it were the last

to listen to the silence of the weary heart

to cherish new friends

to keep old ones within embrace

to sleep on the grass on rainy nights

to read a book with absent pages

to count the teeth of the Water Dragon

to doubt those in power and their flaming tongue

to hoist the Word above the waters

to master every line in the poetry of pain

# SOLACE

*(for Molara whose wise words took away some of Katrina's sting)*

Take heart,
Daddy mine

We lost our house
But not our home

We lost our books
But not our brains

We lost our shoes
But not our feet

We lost our hats
But not our heads

We lost some windows
But not our wind

We lost our wardrobe
But not our clothes

You lost some songs
But not your voice

I regret our loss
I celebrate our LIFE

# KATRINA SNAPSHOTS

*(Overheard at the Evacuation Centres)*

When the levees broke
And the city drowned
The President blamed the Governor
The Governor blamed the Mayor
The Mayor blamed the weather
The weather blamed the sky
The sky blamed the sea
The sea blamed the wind
The wind blamed...


\*          \*          \*


Said Otis, Painter:

The sky this night
is a patchwork
of broken stars
Moontears fall
like famished rain
Somewhere beneath the mud,
my rainbow brush

When Thunder spoke, at last,
its sermon came
in syllable of iron.
Katrina's sky is a
riot of colours
too dense for a prentice canvas

\*     \*     \*

My father was a carpenter
Never owned what he built
My mother was a laundry woman
Whose rugged hands tended
The wardrobe of the very rich

Their proud and favoured son,
I owned the house I built
The clothes I washed
Were those in my very wardrobe

Then Katrina
Un-built my house
Soaked my clothes
In its toxic sludge

The day the levees broke
The floods paved my way
Back to the plantation

\*     \*     \*

Oh Pelican,
Bird of the Swamp
Where are you;
Your tall, thin legs
Your migrant beak?
The lovely mangrove
The imperious cypress
Lament your flight
At the coming of the storm

Come back later
Come back quick
We lost many branches
But our roots still lie deep
In the brackish waters


*         *         *


Said Tyrone, Jazz Pianist

I can hear
the moan of squelching notes
from the distance;
the flood's light-fingered touch
on the keyboard:

the old grand piano
in my living room
must be drowning...


*         *         *


Tamika, Lay Philosopher

Serenaded us about
Booker T who asked
Negroes to use their hands
And Dr. Du Bois who placed
The premium on their brains.

It was night
And the frogs picked up the argument
In a city just re-
Claimed by the swamp

\*        \*        \*

Muses Lamont, Community Activist:

Poverty
is
a
weapon
of
mass
destruction

\*        \*        \*

(At the UNO* Evacuation Centre)

A throng
extracted from flooded holes

Hauled here
by anonymous boats

Reeking
of dirt and rage.

Little brown mounds
litter the seminar rooms

A sickly yellow stream
meanders down the hallway

Needed help
is many Black Hawks away

Here I am,
destitute on a campus

Where three days ago
I was professor of many books.

\*          \*          \*

Ubiquitous Anderson Cooper
Thrashing through the rubble
Camera fixed upon
What they would rather hide

"Third World America"
with half a city
stranded on their roofs

\*University of New Orleans

# IV.

# KATRINA WILL NOT HAVE THE LAST WORD

## ENIA LASOO MI[1]

Uncle Gabriel heard
What Katrina did to our wardrobe
And instantly divined our needs:

A pageant of clothes
Flew fast across the ocean
Sewn with care, embroidered with kindness

Historian, humanist, priest of rigorous virtues
He knows the story of the loom
And our stubborn preference for native fabrics

I donned my new garments
With grateful pride, thumping my
Well-clad nose at Katrina's stripping catastrophe

*Enia lasoo mi*

Babatunde's bundle came
From Ontario rio rio
That generous city where once I swam
In the lake of books and rainbow shoals

Songster, intrepid penman of angry prose,
His smile much kinder than his sarcastic pen
Tunde sent a wardrobe of garments and graceful words

Only this:
His XXL estimate of his old teacher
Was three sizes bigger than his Katrina-harassed girth!

My hands found their way through the sleeves
The way my ears danced through his verse
In the busy workshops of our UI[2] days

*Enia lasoo mi*

Hybrid, high-profile,
The fabrics from Askhari's Alabama loom
Dogon-dyed, Wollof-woven, Yoruba-batiked

Generously loose around the waist
Hugging-tight on the shoulders
Billowy-sleeved, amply embroidered

A happy cotton warms the loom
Of these gifts: freedom-gathered
Joy-ginned, with memory lush

And lusty like the symphony
Of savannah winds
Scalloped skirts, terraced trousers

Bouncing *buba, danshiki*[3] roomy
Like a royal castle; head gear
Rising through the roof, far into the American sky

Kindred Spirit, Daughter of the Nile,
Our gratitude is made of a fabric
That never wears nor tears

*Enia lasoo mi*

---

[1]  People are my clothes – a Yoruba saying
[2]  University of Ibadan
[3]  Two types of loose-fitting garments popular in Nigeria.

*In the order in which they are mentioned in the poem: G.A. Akinola, Babatunde Ajayi,
Askhari Johnson Odari.*

78

# KATRINA WILL NOT HAVE THE LAST WORD

Today
Two brown bundles arrived
From my friends in
The land of France Preseren*,
Rippling with poems and stories
And rippling generosity from
The depth of the Slovene heart

An envelope landed pat
On my vacant desk
Bearing the latest songs
Of Obierika, the master story teller,
With an inscription in
Bold, impeccable lettering:
   "What the storms took away
     friendship will restore"

*Katrina will not have the last word*

Ogun's scion, He-of-the-Fiery-Pen,
Couriered his own munificence and care
From his roost across the seas:
"*O ku ewu*, Niyi**. Take heart.
I took another look at Ahmadu Bello Way
Yesterday, wondering how far we are
From our own Katrina"

*Katrina will not have he last word*

Yet another envelope from
The 'Young Turks' of Nigerian letters,
Bearing the Oil Lamp man's Cornell address
Just one day before the Dadakuada acolyte
Crooned in the message of the Irele clan

A voice rang across the borders
With a deep Arnoldian kindness:
"Just tell me your current address;
We have something here for your urgent need."
I was still wondering how to say 'thank you'
When another envelope couriered in
The boon from the Soji-Sonala campaign
While Dipo (First Class in every aspect)
Called to say his helping hand was on the way
Kalamu ya Salaam networked for our desperate needs,
His voice strong and very wise
The *UP SCHOOL* group rallied round
With gifts and healing words
And gleeful memories of our old Agidimo Values.
From Sweden came a large and lasting gift:
The Apidan scholar discerned our needs
From a long and careful distance
And her helping hand abridged the oceans

*Katrina will not have the last word*

Enter Dave Brinks, Caveat Minstrel
With a bouquet of books
His voice bruised by Katrina's plague,
His songs kind and stronger still
Just like the tall generosity of the Songstress Incognito
Whose box of beneficence came
All the way from her Arizona bounty,
Dancing, still, Beneath the Prairie Moon
She knew we had Enough Pain to Go Round
And dispatched shiploads of urgent balm

When the Dogon Queen
Heard the sermon of the Storm
On the other side of the Mighty Ocean,
The Sable Clan went into action;
A capacious package was soon on the way
Bearing books and other direly needed things.

And the countless kindnesses
Of the Blanton Bunch who brought
Faith and friendship so uniquely close;
Linguists who know the vowel of virtue
Gracious clan of the River-that-Ever-Flows.
The laughters of 14 Heron Street still salute the ear,
Perching like peerless birds on memory's tree

*Katrina will not have the last word*

Bamako Jaji reached out from his Harvard roost,
Humanity's friend, generous as the wind,
Bringing news from the Polyglot by the Garonne,
Caring bridge-builder who followed
Apace with a flotilla of favours;
From the Bearded Sugarman of Ibadan
Came a kindly chattering and soothing song
Then Iwa's clan's tender entreaty
And the therapeutic laughter
Of the Poet Who (Never) Lied

*Katrina will not have the last word*

Little Damilola walked up to me,
His face alive with kindness
"Daddy told me about your many losses;
Our Mistress also did in our poetry class
This is all I have in my piggybank, Sir;
I give it with all respect"

Then this, from a fervent soul
Across the Mighty Ocean:
"Gold and silver have I none,
But in the name of the God I serve
All you lost shall return in multiple folds"

*Katrina will not have the last word*

\*   Slovenia (Preseren is the national poet of that country).
\*\*  Compliments on your survival
In the order in which they are mentioned in this poem, the following benefactors:
Writers and friends from Slovenia, Chinua Achebe, Wole Soyinka, Ogaga
Ifowodo, Abdul Rasheed Na'Allah, Abiola Irele, Steve Arnold, Soji Akinrinade,
Sonala Olumhense, Dipo Adamolekun, Kalamu ya Salaam, Christ's School, Ado
Ekiti Alumni, Kacke Gottrick, Dave Brinks, Cynthia Hogue, Kadija George,
Mackie and Linda Blanton and their daughter Jordan, Biodun Jeyifo, Christiane
Fioupou, Femi Osofisan, Sola Olorunyomi, Odia Ofeimun, Damilola.

## NOAH*

Noah, Noah, what a lark!
Just how large is your little ark?
The tiny pigeon and the crooning dove
Season of kindness and lots of love

Your little ark our friendly roost
Where laughter gives our life a boost
When we were sacked by a vicious flood
And nearly lost our precious blood

In your ark is Autumn, ever kind
A gentler mother is hard to find
And noble Scott who brightens our days
A true new man in many ways

Life to you as you grow and thrive
May your ark get bigger the more you strive

* Young son of Autumn White who, with her partner Scott Neuman, gave my
wife and me refuge in their house in Birmingham, Alabama in the first half of
September 2005

# FOR THE LEMAYS*

Another house – by the lake
Feet washed by laughing ripples
And the ceaseless chuckling

Of dancing ducks
Whirring pines argue overhead
At the wind's insistence;

The maple's many-fingered foliage
Is umbrella without the slightest
Hint of umbrage. Squirrel songs

Rise and ripen with the nuts
The sky eyes the Monadnock
With a northeastern intensity.

Fear no death by water
Lemay said without dismay
There is enough love & laughter here

To disperse that memory of
The deadly storm you left behind.
The lake settles

In the fountain of my pen
My nib glides on mists
And magic mirrors

---

*   whose house on Rocky Road, New Hampshire, became our home from mid-
September 2005 to mid-January 2006. Peter and Andrew Lemay helped gut our
devastated house in New Orleans, and Peter came again to assist with our insur-
ance claims.

# FRANKLIN PIERCE UNIVERSITY

*(Beacon on the mountaintop)*

Lamp, shining bright
from the mountaintop
unhideable like a midday sun

Night passes here
without its darkness
windows glow like fireflies

The Monadnock looms
in the sky, eyes trained
on your fledgling letters

Season after season
young dreams stream up
and down this mountain

Fluid and free
like tadpoles in
your lake beside the road


\*         \*         \*


Franklin speaking,
you gave me

a pen
and a universe of papers

a desk
and waiting chair

hilly walkways
and a community of kindness

My first poem here
is a nest of riffs and ravens

# KNOWING FRIEND

*(for Don Burness*
*for Mary-Lou\*)*

He measures his day
By the volume of my laughter
Studies my looks
Like his book of vital signs

Since Katrina's calamitous coming
He has noticed those vacant lots
In the country of my face
My long, lingering gaze

My absent moments
And those sighs which erupt
From some anguished corner
In the chambers of my heart.

A soft, peripatetic polyglot,
He understands the language
Of loss, brutal bereavements
Violent uprootings, and sudden dis-

Locations. He knows when
Blind storms have shifted the sky,
When houses roam the streets
In search of their missing roofs

He can feel the tremor of the terror
When I struggle to re-call
Favourite lines from a missing book,
The tantalizing phantom of vanished

Manuscripts. He can read
The deep-etched scars of the storm and
Katrina's savage scarification on the
Face of a once serene colleague


\* Great friends through whom we got to know Franklin Pierce
University, and whose genuine love and care cushioned our
Katrina semester in New Hampshire.

# NOW THIS

### i

For the friend
Who called with the following message:

*Hey man, I heard Katrina*
*Washed you out completely.*
*Congratulations! That'll be good stuff*
*For another book of poems...*

### ii

And another
Who shouted this across the distance:

*Hello there*
*We heard you lost everything*
*Just let me know*
*If there is anything you need*
*And if there is anything that I can do...*

# PLACIDO*

Katrina
        came
                saw
but never
                        conquered

When it pulled me deep
Into its fetid jaws
Unstoppable hands reached out
With vital help

Unforgettable, Placido:
True Man of Peace
Christian who carries his Christ
In every act

Artist and artisan
Who wields the hammer
As he hums the hymn
The saw, the box-knife
Pliers, the shearing gear
All which keep his hands and mind
In perpetual engagement
No home, no workplace
Ever looks the same
After Placido's workman magic
His house a cluttered haven
For sundry tools
His old Nissan's roof rack
Is hardly ever free of helpful freight

His "Good morning" is truly good
His "Good night" a friendly invocation
Of the limitless beneficence of angels
Possessing so little,
He is possessed by even less
Average in size and status
Though a big heart beats in his small chest
His broken English sews the garment
Of a tattered world, professes a passion
Whose beauty lies beyond the fabric of words
Life's wheel runs in a careful cycle,
He often says,
Give so much of your breakfast bread
And a bounty may bounce on your dinner table
The more you give
The more you are given
Placido's Cross never cancels the Sacrifice
Caring and sharing are no idle rhymes


\*      \*      \*


Cuba-born, world-wise,
Placido understands the language
Of angry winds
Long schooled in the path of hurricanes
He knows their primal madness

I sing your name, oh Placido
Gentle Warrior, faithful Pilgrim

Earth's friend
Dreamer of laughing skies

Hands versatile as clay
A heart just as supremely tender

Humble as the grass
Which breathes beneath his sole

Yet tall as a tower
Of imperishable virtues

From the crucible of his courage
A thousand eagles leap into the skies

From the calloused pit of his palm
Love rises like much-neaded dough

Weatherer of many seasons
He cracks thunder's code

Knowing full well when the water we drink
Swells rapidly into the flood which consumes us

Those who live by the sea, he said, must
Learn vital lessons from the ambiguity of water

When the sky was sour and the wind
Drove the lake into our inner rooms

Placido's life vests arrived
Later, his rescue boat

Then, the hurray and hunger
Of 'higher grounds'

The miraculous resurrection of those
We thought the water had buried

I sing your name, Placido
Cuba-born, world-embraced

I sing your name
In the pristine theatre of virgin forests

I sing your name
In the open platform of fallowing grasslands

I sing your name
With the ripening roar of fluted pumpkins

I sing your name
To the tuberous promise of leafy groves

I sing your name
To the bounteous banter of teeming barnyards

I, Farmer's Son,
Offspring of the Machete, Scion of the Hoe

Here is my bowl of gratitude
Urgent, full to the brim

\*        \*        \*


'*Pass it on*', you say, Placido
'*Pass it on*'

Those who owe their lives
To the kindness of others
Shouldn't they be eternal
Nurturers of the virtue of giving

Those who live
In the glow of the moon
Shouldn't they for ever pen a paean
To the Mother of Light?

The chain of kindness
Never breaks
The chain of kindness
Never breaks

It may spot a rusty hint
In one little corner
Or suffer a breach
When dropped on a rocky patch


The chain of human kindness
Never breaks

That umbilical cord which binds us all
To the Universal Song
Throbs every moment with
The electricity of Being

The chain of kindness
Never suffers a permanent break

Placido, Friend of the Earth
Confidant of the Sky
I offer Gratitude,
Supreme deity in the pantheon of Virtues


* Neighbour who provided the life vests in which my wife and I swam out of our flooded house, and who boated us out at a time we thought all hope of evacuation and survival was lost.

## WHAT MOTHER SAID

*(Dreamtalk, seven nights after the storm)*

*Omo lakoko ororogiro*
*Omo lakoko meso jobibo*

Pride of my Womb
Son of the Farmer
Whose yam dwarfs the mountain
Son of the strong one
Whose *ada* is larger than the loftiest machete
Offspring of the weaver
Who mistresses the loom and the shuttle's song
Offspring of the Indigo Woman
Whose hands are bluer than the bluest sea

I heard the story
With an ache in my loins
I heard the story
And a thousand porcupines invaded my stomach
The ground shook beneath my feet
My head turned light like a bundle of feathers
I heard how the wind howled
How the rain fell
How the lake breached its wall
Poured into the city
And took your house
I heard why I now owe your life
To the kindness of a godly neighbour
Who never knew who your mother was
And yet strove to save her son

I heard about the undrownable power
Of Kindness, the rhythm of the human heart
Which beats in the chest of the universe
I heard about the flood's savage havoc and asked:
How can Water do this to her own son?
Your losses are many, my son,
Your sadness without compare .
But there is no night so long
That it never ends
No sorrow so deep
It never has its crest of laughter

Walk head up, my Son
Walk head up
As your father once did
As your mother is doing
As we have always taught you to do
A cloudy face does not befit your sky
Stooping shoulders are strange to your gait
Fruit of my Womb
Pride of my prime
You brought me joy in my saddest period
You will not depart my sky like a hasty sun

Son of the Elephant
Son of the Buffalo
Son of the one who shakes the forest
Like a mighty wind
You are no mean subject for the sniggering eye
Son of the Mountain which challenges the sky
Your journey is long
Your destiny distinct
You have ploughed fertile fields
In countless seasons
You will not go the way of the mud
Before the harvestide
Your head was molded from the firmest clay
It will never crack like a paper dome

Obatala is not asleep, my Son
He will never let the work of his hand
Dissolve in a strange and surging flood

Fruit of my Womb
Joy of my life
Osun's precious gift
Her tall, abiding grace
Osun gave you to me
Yes, Osun gave me you
She of the of the soothing voice
And liquid laughter
Eyes like fresh-laid eggs
Lips like well sculpted lobes
She whose beauty is bounty
Skin ebony-black, teeth cotton-white
Wardrobe generous like her supple motions
She of the patient passion, the billowing gaze
Who conquers raging fires with liquid mercies
Parrot feather in Eyekaire's hair
Parrot feathers
Corn-rows with plenteous grains for the looking eye

Parrot feathers in Yeye's hair
Red, red, red like the blood in the season's veins
Dazzling fright to the uninitiated
Unquenchable awe to the marveling acolyte

Parrot feathers
Red like the mystery of the moon
Fertile flow of endless cycles

Parrot feathers
Which tilt the tides and stir the sands

Parrot feathers
Golden glow of burning fancies

Parrot feathers
'Provoke a blaze', declares Eyekaire
Never rest cold with little fires

Fruit of my Womb
Centre of my life
Your coming was never easy
Your birthcry never came before
A long period of tearful silence
My womb was fertile
But death played foul with
The joys in my cradle
Birth after birth after birth
The old robber stole my laughter
Birth after birth after birth
My moments of ululation soon
Gave way to periods of wailing loss
I ran, hands over head, to you. Yeye Osun

You divined my affliction
Even before I had time to open my mouth
*"Soft, soft, is the song of the clay",*
Your voice came, soothing to my panting ears
*"Soft, soft, are the feathers of the pigeon;*
*Cool, ever cool, is the house of the crab*
*The raffia palm draws its wine*
*From a cellar beneath the swamps*
*Freely does the hen dance through a thicket of thorns*
*Freely*
*The duck never goes through life*
*Without a retinue of ducklings*
*The streamside plantain clump*
*Never lacks a tribe of teaming suckers*
*Your egg this time will hatch a chick*
*Too strong for the claws of the hawk*
*The cock which grows from the chick*
*Will be the type that crows*
*From the top of the tallest roof.*

*Walk quietly back home*
*Continue in all your virtues*
*Let compassion be your closest company*
*For she who casts cool water on the road ahead*
*Will never walk on scalding earth*

*Olomi is the name of the child in your future*
*In his infant years, he will swallow no pill*
*Or drain the cup of alien brew*
*Water will be his herb*
*Water his all-round cure*
*Whenever fever comes with its shivering fire*
*Invoke my water and rout the foe…*
*Cool, ever cool, is the house of the crab"*

Eyekaire never went back on her promise
You waded strong and wise in her waters
The fish your friend,
The pigeon your favourite bird
You flowed back and forth
Like her famous water
Every healthy coast your consort
The valley your lofty roost
You sang the rainsong everywhere you went
You never broke your covenant with Water

\*            \*            \*

Fruit of my Womb
Eyekaire gave you to me
How can the fetid waters of another land
Take you away from her vigilant hands?
*Eewo!*

Pride of my life
I shower you with my blessings
Pride of my life
I fortify you with my prayers

You will not stumble when you walk
You will never choke
On the water of the Living Spring
Whatever way heads to the house of greatness
May your feet stay steady on its happy lane
You are my streamside shrub and towering *iroko*
No wind will diminish the majesty of your height

    Freely does the hen dance
    Through a thicket of thorns
    Freely

You are the shining lamp
On crest of my hill
No native foe will dim you light
No alien force will shrink your reach

I touch my womb this day
So many seasons after
My body aches at the news of your losses
My knees wobble, my teeth clatter
At the hearing of your cry
Crimson waters of the beginning
Crimson waters of Breaking Moments
Pulsing dawns, bleeding twilights
Cradling oceans, inchoate skies
New-laid eggs, warm and wary
Cosmic crack of breaking shells
Thin-legged stagger of fledgling gaits
Frantic fancy of first feathers
The fright before the flight
The ultimate navigation
Of the waters of the wind
Mapless journeys, itinerant dreams
Sedentary pods, flying seeds
Way-wide rainbow across the sky…

Freely does the hen dance
Through a thicket of thorns
Freely

May your path be clear
Pride of my prime
May your path be clear
The eagle finds its niche on the tallest tree
When the earthworm pays its homage
The earth opens its door for it
The sea may seethe/boil
The lake may swell
Oluibu will find her way
Through the wildest waters

Freely does the hen dance
Through a thicket of thorns
Freely

Fruit of my Womb
The eyes watching you are many
The eyes watching you are many
Olosunta never sleeps in his majestic heights
Oroole's rescue hands are long and strong
Osun ripples on
In the valley beneath their shadows
Her vigilant water astir in our veins
The eyes watching you are many
Pride of my prime
The eyes watching you are many
Your limbs are tributaries of a generous river
No alien floods will stem your flow

Freely does a hen dance
Through a thicket of thorns
Freely

Joy of my life
The stories I hear are truly grave
Your losses are many
Your privations are countless
"My books, my books, my books!",
You intone in a voice heavy with pain
"My vital papers, my half-formed songs,
My dreams-in-progress
My sunny nights, my star-lit days
My fountains of memory, my magic and my muse
The tools of my trade, the tales of my toil
My fiercely guided wealth,
The leaves of my Living Tree "
My wife's priciest possessions
Those piggybanks of memory that were
Treasure troves of the children experience...

Salt of my sea
I hear your voice, I feel your pain
I was never blind to your love of the book
I have seen you protect a piece of paper
As a lion protects its cub
I have seen you journey a thousand miles
For the sake of a rare pamphlet
I have seen you crouched at your desk
From sunup to sundown
Reading and writing
Reading and writing again
I have seen you talk with books
Standing prosperously in your shelves
The way champion yams jostled for
Space in your father's barn
Books are your friends
Books are your flair
Books are your consort
Books are your comfort
From the ones which sprawl
On your desk like murmuring mountains

To the *konkolo* ones which live
In your breast pocket
Books are holy guests and hosts
In your house
Always there in your sitting room
There on the kitchen table
There by the bedroom window
There in the little room
Where you sing even when you squat
Right on the stoop beside the painted railing
They talk with you while eating
You talk back in your sleep
You chew them like the sage's kola nuts
They drill your ignorant moments
They tumble down with your morning shower
They are the aroma of your favourite dish
They are the silent sound of your laughter
They are the stanzas in your song of sorrow
Brick by vital brick
They are the walls of your House of Life
Your loom of endless yarn

    Freely does the hen dance
    Through a thicket of thorns
    Freely

Pride of my life
I know your loss
I feel your pain
But eloquent as books are
They cannot say *E kaa ro*
When they see me in the morning
They cannot say *okun o*
When I stub a toe
Wise as they are
They cannot provide the coffin
For my last journey

Honey of my hive
I know what is gone
My heart aches for what is missing
But here is what my mother said
The day I lost my only daughter:

| | |
|---|---|
| *Omi nii danu* | Only the water has spilled |
| *Uwowoo fo* | The gourd is still intact |
| *Erun oko ni ya sonu* | The hoe has lost its blade |
| *Alagbede ti ku* | But the blacksmith is still alive |

There is no night so dark
That it does not end in some kind of dawn
No sorrow so profound
That it does not leave room
For a few streaks of laughter
Look through the window
Of your house of sadness
Behold the lawn and the sprouting grass
The dust on the road
As it rises—and falls
The roar of traffic
And the silence in between
The leaves on the great *odan* tree
As they move to the music of the wind
Listen to the funeral toll of the nearby church
The boisterous bell of the school playground
Behold the buffalo which says
Its head is an unbearable burden
And the crab which says it has none to call its own
Trace Life's long journey
Through the lines on your palm
Count your teeth with the tip
Of your tongue
Place your hand on the left part of your chest
That magic throbbing there is your vital gift
Never let the flood that took your books away
Come near the pump of that amazing engine.

Freely does the hen dance
Through a thicket of thorns
freely

Sun of my Sky
You are not alone
Callers throng your door
With greetings and prayerful wishes
Some bringing gifts
Some with valuable replacements
For your missing things
Some with songs rooting you
To a happier earth
Steadying you in the saddle
Of your horses of memory
Some simply humming your Songs of Hope
The bird in your favourite tree
Chirruped your name yesterday
The earthworm heard the tune
And told the soil

Freely does then hen dance
Through a thicket of thorns
Freely

You are not alone
Beloved Son of mine
You are not alone
The bamboo clump never lacks a throng of shoots
You are not alone, my son
People are your clothes
So discard the hurricane's drenched rags
Slay its stench
Unclaw its grip
Let your tears dry with the floods
Stride out of the mud,
Your arms swinging by your side
Courage your company

Laughter your lyric
Sing your songs as never before
*Ule oba ko jo*   When the palace burns down
*Ewa nibu si*   It is only asking for a more beautiful replacement
You are not alone

    Freely does a hen dance
    Through a thicket of thorns
    Freely

Pride of my Life
Was it not just one moon ago
That the world gathered
At the fireplace of your voice
Was it not just one moon ago
That I sat, head high,
In your hall of honour
My eyes bright, my heart glowing
My mind spinning as my *akeke* did
In my days at the loom


My boy stood tall
    Just like his father

His eyes sparkled with life
    Just like his father's

His voice was honey
    Just like his father's

His words cut like a whetted machete
    Just like his father's

His face black like *koro usin*
    Just like his father's

His teeth white like the egret
Just like his father's

His sadness seething and strong
Just like his father's

His laughter loud and deep
Just like his father's

His friends many and gracious
Just like his father's

His foes mean and sneaky
Just like his father's

His heart large and vulnerable
Just like his father's

His mind free and fertile
Just like his father's

His stubbornness strong and steady
Just like his father's

His tenacity firm like ardent glue
Just like his father's

Freely does a hen dance
Through a thicket of thorns
Freely


Friend of my Dawn
I touched my head seven times
Fell on my knees seven times
In awe of She-of-the-Wonder-Water

*Ore o ore o*
*Ore Yeeeeye o*

I felt Eyekaire's intimations
In the pit of my memory
I pledged seven white kola nuts
To the Mother of the River
Three ripe *orogbo* to Ifa,
Father of Sooth and Wisdom
Who foretold your coming
I promised Mother Earth
Nine long shadows and a bowl of dew
I promised the four hundred deities
A bucket of songs and an acre of dance
Spare his life, I prayed,
Let this one live beyond my twilight

I am still ready to serenade the stars
From now till tomorrow morning
Light every night with the lantern of my moon
Feed a thousand pigeons
Spend endless days on the bank of the Great River…
I will do anything, son
To make sure your days on earth
Are longer than mine
The sun which light my sky so bright
Will not set in the middle of its day
The glorious feather in my plume
Will not be plucked by hawkish death

    Freely does the hen dance
    Through a thicket of thorns
    Freely

Oh you Rocks, you Rivers
Esidale, Spirit of *Ori* and Origins
Orunmila, Father of Sooth and Truth
Iyami Iyami, you Wonder-birds that fly without wings

You dust of the sky that settles
In the backyard of the moon
You who broke the Word like ripened kola
With the mandate of your teeth
You who spread the sky like an umbrella
The earth like a mat from sea to sea

*Awoyaaya loju aye*   The one that breaks open in the eyes of the
　　world
*Adikunkun dikunku lule Orunmila*   One that is wrapped in
　　absolute mystery in the house of Orunmila
*Adiitu, adiimo bi omi agbon*   Mysterious like the water inside the
　　coconut
*Oyi re re re re*   Winds like merciful breezes

　　Freely does the hen dance
　　Through a thicket of thorns
　　Freely

Clay of the Beginning
Soft, sensible medium
Of moulding Mothers
You whose ears are tuned
To the poetry of the palm
Spirit of Singing Waters
Spirit of the Wind
Spirit of Her who was
Before the birth of time
Secure his feet on Life's path

　　Freely does the hen dance
　　Through a thicket of thorns
　　Freely

Pride of my prime
Your days will be long
*Orii faun*   The tortoise never suffers a headache
*Edo i rin gbin*   Nausea never afflicts the snail

*Otutu i meja lale odo* The fish never suffers a chill in the depth of
  the river
*Omo Omi* Child of Water
*Omo Omi* Child of Water
*Omo Omi e gbedo bo'do lo* The child of the River is never wasted
  by the River
*Mo de loni o* Here I come again
*Ore Yeeye Osun* Osun, Mother of Virtues
*Opo ule mi lee yi* This is the pillar of my house
*Moo je ye* Do not let it fall

Eyekaire, Mother of Mercy
You gave him to me
When my day was young
Secure him, prolong his days
Let him be there to close my eyes
When my long journey has come to its end

    Freely does the hen dance
    Through a thicket of thorns
    Freely

---

*Omolakoko ororogiro* Son of owners of the fruit-laden akoko tree
*Omolakoko meso jobibo* Whose fruits are big like the ginning slab
*Ada:* Machete, cutlass
*Osunn:* Goddess of River Osun; also known as Eyekaire (The-Mother-we-adore)
*Eewo:* Abomination, taboo
*Iroko:* Tropical tree common in the rainforest area of Nigeria; regarded as the king
  of trees
*Oluibu:* Lord of the Oceans
*Konkolo:* small
*E kaa ro:* Good morning
*Okun o:* A common Ekiti-Yoruba greeting used in all kinds of situations—expres-
  sion of sympathy, affection, solidarity, etc

*Odan:* An evergreen leafy tree whose shade provides meeting spots in town and
villages

*Akeke:* Spindle

*Koro isin:* seed of the akee; glowingly black

*Ore o ore o:* Favour favour

*Ore Yee yeee o:* Favour of the Great Mother (Osun)

*Orogbo:* bitter kola.

# V.

# AFTERWORD

# THIS CITY WILL NOT DIE*

And yet
This city will *not* die

Though prostrate now from
The poison of pestilential floods

And levees which toy with
The murderous fury of raging waters;

Footless floodwalls, the dirt and dust
Of dykes which humour the hubris

Of the lake... Lost lanes. Beaten boulevards
And the Crescent City sprang a breach

In its arc. Sick now, my favourite pharmacy,
Starved, that grocery store which once stunned my gaze

With sheer cornucopia. Pale, the pump
Kin colour on the face of the moon

The museum has lost its muse
The library its lore of letters

But sick, not dead,
This betrayed City

Deserted,
Not forgotten

I can hear drumtaps in the distance
The sexy serenade of the sax-o-phone

Rainbow umbrellas in the evening sky
The penitent after-Mass of Fat Tuesdays

Flood-scorched trees will bloom again
The wounded oak will stretch its limbs

Even as the winds stir its mossy beard
The birds, long gone, will return to roost

As gumbo revelers sweeten up
The laughter of the streets

This City will rise again
This Big (Un)Easy, this neglected treasure

\*   Originally performed August 29, 2006, at the University of New Orleans first anniversary commemoration of the Katrina disaster.

## NEW ORLEANS IS

New Orleans is
Humanity, Music, and Desire

New Orleans is
Agriculture, Piety, and Abundance

New Orleans is
Art, Felicity, and Fidelity

New Orleans is
Treme, Bourbon, and Congo Square

New Orleans is
Wildair, Warrington, and Wickfield

New Orleans is
Pelican, Heron, and Flamingo

New Orleans is
Charity, Gentilly, and Saratoga

New Orleans is
Black Street, White Street, and Gray Boulevard

New Orleans is
Gumbo, Jambalaya, and Red Beans 'n Rice

New Orleans is
Juice, jive, and jolly jazz

New Orleans is
River, Lake, and Ocean

New Orleans is
Sounds, Saints, and Sinners

New Orleans is
Love, tears, and laughter

New Orleans is
People

# INTERVIEW

# NEW ORLEANS IS PEOPLE

## Niyi Osundare Interviewed by Rebeca Antoine

*This interview is dedicated to my wife, Kemi, whose strength and courage made it possible for us to survive that terrible sojourn in the attic.*

Niyi Osundare, a Nigerian poet and professor, was teaching at the University of New Orleans at the time of Katrina. He and his wife were forced into their attic by the rising waters and were eventually rescued by a neighbor.

**When did you first hear about Hurricane Katrina?**

Like all the others in New Orleans, about four days before it actually hit. I think that was when it was still lingering on the Atlantic, before it entered the Gulf. Of course the warnings and announcements became intensified once it was in the Gulf barrelling towards New Orleans. And about two days before it landed, both the mayor and the governor were talking about evacuation. But it wasn't 'til a couple hours before the hurricane that they started talking about mandatory evacuation. So, like all the others in New Orleans, we, too, were glued to our television. We knew it was coming.

**Were you worried about it?**

Absolutely. Oh, yes. Nobody could have seen—could have heard—that that kind of storm was coming without getting worried, especially considering the havoc it wrought in Cuba, Jamaica, and some Caribbean Islands that it passed through. So, we were worried. I'm sure that your next question will be, "Why didn't you evacuate?"

**Did you think about evacuating?**

We did, but my wife and I had a daughter with us. She's our deaf girl. We wanted to get her out first. She was going back to Gallaudet University in Washington. So, Saturday morning, very early, my wife took her—tried to get her to the airport. There was such a massive traffic backup that she missed her flight. We couldn't even get to the airport.

We had to return home. So, Sunday morning at three my wife took her out, and eventually she left that day. By the time she left, it was already too late for us to evacuate. And then, my wife also worked at Charity Hospital, and she thought she might be called because she was put on—I don't know what they call it—some kind of emergency. And if she was called, and if she had to leave, that I would go with her and shelter at Charity. So, that was why; we were waiting for the call, and then the wind started getting stronger and stronger.

**When was that?**

The hurricane came on Monday. That was Sunday before the hurricane came. It became impossible for us to leave the house, really, when the winds kept coming.

**Where's your home?**

5317 Wickfield Drive. Very close to the campus [UNO] here. That's between Filmore and Prentiss. Or something like that. It's quite close to this place. That's where we were. That's how it met us at home. When the wind came, it was very furious. But it only removed a few shingles from our roof. It wasn't until about nine o'clock, nine-thirty, on the 29th. That's Monday, when the water started coming.

**Is that in the morning?**

In the morning, yes. My wife looked through the window and said, "Oh, my God, what kind of water is this?" Before we knew what was happening, it was on our driveway. Before we knew where we were, it was under the house, and it started lifting the carpet, you know.

So, we were looking for all kinds of places to put our things. Normally, my wife and I had books, things, all over the place. The shelf couldn't take everything, and I'm not a terribly tidy person as far as keeping books and papers is concerned because I always like to see the books I'm reading. I like to see them physically. So, I have so many—I had so many books—close to, I mean, by my bedside. All those ones were the first to go.

And then: One foot. Two feet. Three feet. Four feet. And it was so rapid. And the current was also rapid, what we had in our house.

It was at that point we were trying to rescue all we could, trying to put all those things on the lower shelves right onto the higher shelves. That didn't work because the shelves started falling into the water. It was at that point my wife then said, "Niyi, we are going to drown."

I don't know why it didn't occur to me. I was so consumed by the anxiety to rescue as many of my books and documents as possible; of course I couldn't really rescue them. I began to wonder, "Where do we go from here?"

So my wife said, "Attic. Let's go to the attic." We had never opened the attic ourselves. It was the Terminix man who usually came, and I watched him one or two times when he had to go up the attic, so I tried to do what I saw him do, you know, it took quite some time. The stairwell fell into the river, and so we climbed up the ladder. There were about eight rungs to the ladder. The water went up as far as the sixth. So, we were sitting there near the edge, and our feet were in the water. We were watching the water rise on the 29th, afternoon, evening, and then night. Night was terrible. It was dark, and I was able to go up the attic with a torch, a flashlight, and my wife also was able to save her cell phone, put it between her teeth as we went up. And then, my small transistor radio. We also had my small transistor radio, and we could at least hear what was happening. Many of the radio stations were broadcasting. On it we heard people shouting "Oh, the water is rising. My uncle has drowned." My wife and I took turns, at night, to fix the light on the water. It was rising. We were so scared that it might rise, swallow us where we were, and choke us. It was a really scary night.

And about 5:30 that morning, the torch [flashlight] went out. I think it just burnt out. But it had served us. Now, we were able to make it through the night. Of course, no food, no water... Nothing.

And then we began to wonder, what's going to happen today? We were hungry. We were thirsty. We were tired. But even beyond that: can we survive another night in this kind of place? No.

And, of course, all along we were calling 911. And getting all kinds of responses, you know. I think we called five times.

The fifth time a lady picked up the phone and asked where we were. I told her where we were.

She said, "How old are you?"

I don't know what that has to do with our plight. We told her how old we were, and she said, "Go out in a boat."

And I told her, "There is no boat here. None at all."

I asked her in utter desperation: "How can we get one?"

"I don't know," she answered.

So I asked her, "A whole city is underwater? And there is no boat?"

This was at 2:30 in the night. And she said, "Okay. You stand on your roof and the helicopter might see you."

I said, "How can a helicopter see me at 2:30 in the night? And how many helicopters anyway?"

One or two was hovering above our head. Maybe, we heard their rumbling once every two hours. Something like that. And besides, we couldn't cut a hole through the roof. There was nothing to use, you know. We had no hatchet. And why wasn't there a hatchet in the attic? Because we had never been in that kind of situation before.

The fifth time we didn't actually complete the phone call when everything just went silent. "Brmp." I think it was at that time that the telephone system in New Orleans gave up. So, from that time on, we had no contact at all with the outside world. No contact at all. It was scary. I mean, everywhere around us was water. We didn't know what was happening out there. And I don't know what kept us going. Somehow we kept hoping that something might happen. Nothing happened for a long, long time. My wife and I were shouting occasionally, "Help. Help!" But as time went on, our strength diminished, and we couldn't even shout. There was a hammer. Some little hammer there in the attic. And I looked for a metal object. I hit the hammer on the object so as to produce some noise, some SOS sound, at least to let people know we were there. We don't know whether there was anybody around anyway. About four or five o'clock the following day... that was, oh God... **Wednesday or Tuesday?**

No, on Tuesday. The hurricane was, the 29th? Tuesday, yes, on Tuesday afternoon. It was hot in the attic. Extremely hot. And the attic is where you keep all these insulation materials and so on. Yes, these materials were soaking up every bit of oxygen around and releasing heat. So we couldn't breathe. And my wife started running out of breath and gasping. I, too, started gasping. It was at that point I really got scared because I thought we were going to choke to death.

At this point, the water had stopped rising, but we had between eight and nine feet of water in our house. Now we had no air. No oxygen.

Miraculously, my wife said she heard a sound on the roof. I thought it was hallucination. But it wasn't. It was Placido Sabalo, our Cuban-American neighbor. He came to his house to see if he could rescue anything but discovered he couldn't because the whole place was taken up by water. He was on his way back when he heard our sound. So he traced us to our place. He rescued us. My wife and I owe our lives to this kind neighbor.

On Monday morning, when the water had just started rising, and was about two feet or so in our house, Placido and I kept on talking on the phone, and he told me if we needed anything we should let him know. About an hour later ,when the water had risen by about six inches, he came over to our house to see how things were going.

He came back again and said, "This is very bad water. A very bad storm."

And then it was raining. He gave my wife and me two life jackets. I almost said, "Oh, no, don't worry. I don't think this is necessary." Reluctantly, we took the two life jackets, and he put on the third. With a sword in his hand, and looking like a warrior, he jumped into the rapidly rising flood, waded off, and disappeared We didn't see him until the day after, and that was when he came on a rescue mission. When he came back the following day, the water in our house was between eight and nine feet high. Those jackets proved extremely useful.

From the roof, Placido shouted, "Professor, you are here?"

I said, "Yes."

"Come out. Go into boat. Go into boat. Small, small," he said. "You still have life jacket?"

And I said, "Yes."

I fitted the jacket. I fitted one for my wife. I told my wife, "You wait first. Let me go. Let me go first." So, I jumped into the water. Of course, my sofa, my—all our things were bouncing around in the... I had to make my way through.

Then I got to the door and discovered I couldn't open it because of the water pressure, and Placido and another guy in the boat were very anxious. "Get out! Get out! You know, uh, if gas finish, we die." Somehow I was able to force the door, but I could only get it open to a certain extent. When I was trying to crawl out of this small space the only shirt I had got torn. Happened to my wife, too. So, both of us left our house in a short and shirt. No shoes. None at all. They got us on the boat. We looked all around. Where do we go? The whole of New Orleans was underwater anyway.

We were boated off to St. Raphael's Catholic mission on Elysian Fields. It was impossible to recognize our neighborhood. I couldn't see a thing. We couldn't believe it. This was the same place where three days ago the children were playing.

There were so many other evacuees there. The place was crowded. Nothing to eat. Nothing to drink. Well, at least we were there, and we had people to talk to.

**How many people do you think were there?**

Must have been up to two hundred. That's a small place. In a small room. It was tragic. Children. Men. Women. Old people.

The following morning, a few boats came and took us out of the place. First, they landed us at Save-A-Center on Leon Simon. As we rowed by, I discovered that the University of New Orleans was dry—a happy surprise. The irony is that I had thought the university would be vulnerable because of its closeness to the lake; so I transferred my valuable literary documents and materials from there to my house. Of course, the water found them there and destroyed them. I was so happy the university was safe. Then I kept on wondering about water's logic. It went by this university that was so close to it and came right down to those of us that were far.

We were in front of Sav-A-Center for a couple of hours. Then one or two members of the National Guard came. And they took us to the new Kirschman building. When we got there we saw hundreds and hundreds of people. I couldn't recognize that hall, the way it was used. I said, my God, almost another tragic irony. Now I'm a shirtless, nameless, penniless evacuee on the same university where I used to be a professor. So, we're there. Nothing to eat.

**So you still haven't eaten in…?**

No. Nothing to eat. At about nine o'clock. That was September. I don't remember the date now. September 1st or 2nd. They started dropping MRE's. It took some time before we knew how to handle them. They had the water, and they set it down. That was on the third day after the storm hit.

Then we kept wondering, "Are we going to be here forever?" And we were told no, no, no; they were coming to take us to higher ground—that the helicopters were coming. It wasn't until the fourth day that the helicopters started coming. By then they would make one or two sorties and disappear. They would come at nine in the morning and tell you, "Oh, yeah, we're coming at eleven." We would never see them, you know. And we—we were all made to line up. Fifteen to each line, because the helicopter could only take fifteen. We waited and waited. Eventually, the helicopter came. We were packed in like sardines.

When you were here at UNO, you said you didn't have any food until they started bringing the MRE's. Was there any place to lie down, sit down?

The fields. The fields. That was where we slept. Oh yeah, one evening we slept in the corridor. Everywhere was taken. Everywhere! Lecture halls. Don't talk about the restrooms. Oh, no, no, no, no. I don't want to remember their state. Oh my god, it was terrible. I mean, the smell. The stench everywhere. And of course, after people had fouled up the restrooms they started fouling up their surroundings. People were reduced to the state of nature. You would see people as you were passing, especially when it was fairly dark. You would see them pull down their pants and do it— right there—on the field. Right there in the back of the Kirschman building.

It was terrible. Really, really, terrible. So, the helicopter took us— maybe on the fourth day— to Causeway in Metairie. You know, higher ground. We spent the whole day there. It was there we saw the evacuees from other parts of New Orleans. We spent the whole day there, and the buses started coming. We didn't know where they would be taking us. But eventually my wife and I got on a bus which took us to the airport: New Orleans Airport. We spent another night at the airport. Nowhere to sleep, you know. Nowhere to even sit. You had to struggle to find a place on the floor where you could even sit and rest your back against the wall. I had never seen that kind of crowd at the airport before. The following morning the police came, and they started to do crowd control. C30 airplanes, the green one came, and they started batch by batch. We got onto one of the planes.

And I asked, "Where are we going?"

"You just sit. We take you wherever we find space."

About one and a half hours later, the plane landed. I looked around, and I said, "This is Birmingham, Alabama;" I told my wife because I had been there two times before for reading and speaking engagements. I said, "It's Birmingham, for goodness sake." And, indeed, it was Birmingham, Alabama.

From there I was so weak they had to take me in an ambulance to the University of Alabama Teaching Hospital where I was treated for dehydration. They gave me water, something to eat. My wife and I went to the Red Cross Center. Hundreds and hundreds and hundreds of people. At the Red Cross Center we all had to line up. We were processed. We were given bands to tie around our wrists. Identification tags. There were hundreds of cot beds. And who were we to complain? At least we had something to sleep on, a rare luxury. It was there we had our first hot meal in days. And a real good shower. The first time in about a week that we could brush our teeth. We also had access to TV in the hall, and we saw other evacuees on the screen. And we kept wondering, "How long are we going to be here?"

While all this was happening, e-mails were flying all over the place from people who cared about our welfare and wondered about our whereabouts. Hotel accommodations in different cities had been arranged; flight bookings had been done. But no one knew where we were, and we never knew of these generous gestures from friends and high school alumni, particularly Christ's School Alumni, until much later.

After two days at the Red Cross Center, a young couple named Autumn White and Scott Neuman—plus their boy Noah—came to us and said they would like to adopt us. They said they had a house and plenty of room. We said, "Okay, we'll think about it. Let's meet tomorrow." The following day they came back. My wife and I had made up our minds: we would go with them because they were very genuine. So we went with them. They gave us a place in their basement. Occasionally we went to the Red Cross Center to eat, and then we would come back. Now, for the first time in about 10 days I had access to a laptop. It was when I opened my email box that I saw so many messages. About 1,500 messages from all over the world. There were people that were anxious to know where I was.

The Nigerian community in Mississippi, Alabama, and Tennessee got to know what was happening, and they started coming and sending messages and so on. Many Nigerians in Birmingham traced us to where we were, and took care of us in several ways. There was an attempt to make us feel at home. But we had no identity. Nobody knew who we were, so we could not enjoy some of the facilities they were providing other evacuees. We couldn't even get the food stamps because we were like imposters. One afternoon, a young man, Rev. Korubo, and his wife, Bola, both Nigerians, came and saw what was happening. The man left, went to the library in Birmingham, Googled me, and came back with about eight pages. When he showed those at the registeation desk, everybody was like, "Why didn't you tell us you are a poet? Why didn't you tell us you are a professor? Why didn't you…" And I said, "What? I mean, I can't have it written on my forehead." Those papers became our ID. With them we were able to get food stamps. We were able to receive some kind of allowance, some kind of token, usable only at Wal-Mart. So, that was Birmingham.

Oh, while we were still in Birmingham, the Wole Soyinka Society advertised the OSUNDARE RELIEF FUND on their listserv for people to send in their widow's mites. Christ's School Alumni also rallied round with valuable support. Help came from many people in different parts of the world. Constantly people were being informed of what was happening to us, people on that listserv. So, it was they who told the rest of the world that indeed we were safe. And, of course I did a short note, which I sent to them, which they then passed on to other parts of the world. Eventually all Nigerian newspapers carried the story, and at last people at home knew my wife and I were safe. And then I kept on wondering, where do we go from here? No job. No house. No ID. Then a letter came from Franklin Pierce College (now University), very heart-warming, offering me a position as Visiting Professor and Poet in Residence for the Katrina semester, and promising some comfort for me and my wife, away from the eye of the storm. Three years earlier the university had awarded me an honorary doctorate, so I had some kind of relationship with the college. It was called college, then. The friend that facilitated my relationship with the university is Don Burness. He's a poet and an academic. He's retired now. We got that letter, and it was such a relief. But, how do we get to New Hampshire? We had no ID, and in post 9/11 America, you couldn't pass through the airports without a solid ID. We wrote back, and they made arrangements with the airline. The airline allowed us free passage; that was how we left Birmingham for Rindge in New Hampshire, where we were very warmly received. The university provided us a car. We used it for the three months we were there. Then, a couple, Peter and Jean Lemay contacted the university and offered us their house by the lake. We didn't pay a penny, you know. They didn't only give us a place to live.

They provided a lot of warmth, a lot of friendship. We got to know their family.

Peter Lemay is a business man, very articulate, and the wife, the wife is a great lover of literature, especially poetry. They made life really comfortable for us. It was quite painful when we had to leave. Some people felt I should have stayed on, but I couldn't abandon the University of New Orleans to the post-Katrina trauma because the university didn't abandon me in my hour of need in 1997 when we had to bring our deaf daughter back to the US for educational reasons. A job offer from UNO made my family's relocation possible.

We came back in January 2006, and New Orleans was a swamp. A mighty, smelly swamp. I'd never seen something like that before. The trees were dead. The houses—there was the stench of death and decay everywhere. It took me quite some time before I got to our house—or our former house: a place where all we used to own lay buried. It was very difficult. But our story with the Lemays has not ended. Mr. Lemay and his son and his friend's son actually came, and they were in New Orleans for about one week getting out all the dirt and decaying things in the house. I couldn't believe it. He used his contacts to get others to come. Another group came. Yet another group came until the whole place was empty. And then when we had problems with our insurance company, Mr. Lemay also came from Massachusetts. He lives in Andover, in Massachusetts. He came down from there to broker an agreement, literally, between us and the insurance company. We were able to get some money from them because those guys were saying it was flood that damaged our house, not wind, whereas, we're insured for wind and water. So, it's amazing, the kind of friendship that we discovered, and the kind of hospitality, and the kind of good will that we enjoyed all over the place. This took some of the sting of Katrina away. Coming back here was a challenge, a big challenge. We had nowhere to live in New Orleans.

But two Nigerian friends, Rev. Sola Falodun and Phanuel Egejuru, a professor of English at Loyola University New Orleans, got us a trailer at the Episcopal Church on Canal Street where we stayed from mid-January until early February . The Church people were kind, caring, and generous. But the trailer was cold, and most times we ran out of gas. Gas-hunting became a task for my wife and me. Teaching and the reality of our Katrina losses confronted me with a rude bang. For the first time, I realized what it meant to be a professor without books. Difficult semester, very challenging. All my books, all my records, all my lecture notes gone. All my literary correspondences gone. I felt stripped and dispossessed. Many of my students also had similar experiences. We were a community of deprived survivors.

Would you say the university was really the impetus for you to come back to New Orleans? Do you think that if your job wasn't here that you would've returned?

I must say that it's a combination of my love for this city and a love for the university. There is no other city that I've been to in the U.S. that's been like New Orleans. This city has a certain passion about it. It generates its own passion, and it has a way of generating that passion in other people. It's unique, which is why I was surprised when some people were saying New Orleans was not salvageable, therefore, just forget New Orleans and tell New Orleanians to move to other places so that this place could go back to the swamp as it was in the beginning. This city is a very important part of U.S. history, a very important part of the world's cultural landscape. So I returned here— the two forces were the university and the city. On one side I must say that people rose to the challenge in different ways. It was also a very instructive experience for me. The English department, for example, is the largest department in the university. It was amazing how Peter Schock was able to run a whole department on a laptop from an abandoned warehouse in Illinois; how he was able to galvanize people and strengthen our storm-tossed spirits. This was symbolic of what happened at the general university level. It is to our eternal credit that the university never lost the Katrina semester. The challenge was tremendous, and the university met it bravely in many ways.

I wish the American government had been equally forthcoming. I'm somewhat disappointed at the federal government's response to Katrina, first, when it happened, and then the aftermath. It was extremely dispiriting seeing the different universities jumping over one another, eliminating academic programs, cutting jobs, downsizing in very hurtful ways, just managing to hang in there. It was multiple jeopardy for many of the Katrina victims. You lost everything you owned to

Katrina, and now you also lost your job. I know how hard things were, but I was thinking some solid, comprehensive rescue plan should have been extended to educational institutions in New Orleans. America is capable of doing it. Money's not the issue. I put it down to lack of care. Afterall, Katrina was not a totally natural disaster. No. The water that took away everything we had, that nearly took our lives, came from a broken levee. That is the London Avenue Canal. I didn't even know this until months later, that that was where the levee broke and soaked us all in water.So,they should have built a stronger levee and prevented that catastrophe. The government failed in one of its cardinal responsibilities—the protection of human lives and property. It should have made up for this with a salvage plan for the universities. Compulsory downsizing did a lot of damage that would take the institutions years to recover from. It's all very painful.

It seems all the universities here, especially the University of New Orleans, of course, are still recovering from that and from the loss of enrollment.

It's going to take a long time. In fact, I'm surprised at the way we've been able to heal. UNO was lucky that we didn't get water. I mean if you go to SUNO now or to Dillard, those people were soaked. You know what it means for the first floor of a university library or the computer section to go? The losses were devastating, which is why I also feel that more help should have been extended to us here. We needed it.

The city as a whole has lost a lot. Just see the ragged, boarded-up houses, the empty streets, the silent boulevards. For example, the African, especially Nigerian, community in New Orleans has literally disappeared. Makes me so lonesome most times. Yes, this city should have received more help. It deserves it.

It's not just the French Quarter that is New Orleans. No. Not just the tourist areas. New Orleans is people.

And it seems that prior to Gustav there was a lot of anxiety amongst, obviously, the population itself. It seems like there's a lot of anxiety that another Katrina could happen.

Oh, yes. Once it has happened to you and it has scarred you so deeply, it's natural for you to feel like, "Oh, well, I hope another one is not coming." Every potential hurricane or every potential storm gathering on the Atlantic now is more or less a potential Katrina until it proves otherwise. I believe that this city needs to be secured.

It really needs to be secured. Just see all the steel and metal pylons now being driven into the earth to replace the mud and earth levees of the past. In the immediate period after Katrina, there was noise all over the place, the "ba dung, ba dung, ba dung" sound of heavy machinery. You wonder: why was all his not done before now? Why did it take an apocalyptic catastrophe of Katrina's magnitude to remind government about the necessity of a flood-control wall and metal levee around the UNO side of the Lake? I have never stopped asking myself, "Why wasn't this done fifty years ago or one hundred years ago?" Or whatever. New Orleans has been exposed, so dangerously exposed to the elements; we were lucky that the casualties were not more. This is a city that needs to be protected, and America can do it. A country that puts men and women on the moon should be able to secure the rest of us on earth. Flood walls. Solid. Impregnable. High levees. In the past, people put mounds and mounds of earth at the edge of the lake, and they called it a levee, you know. I think the government underestimated the fury of water, and also the anger of water. Water doesn't like to be underestimated. No. It doesn't like to be disdained. And I think that was what happened. We need the levees to be stronger; they will need to be higher. What we have at the moment can't go beyond a Category 2. Anyway, a strong Category 2 will top this and hit the city again. I believe that we should not succumb to a false sense of security. The yearly lull, when November has come and the hurricane season is gone, we tend to forget that June is on its way back again. I have been to Holland, and I know that most of that country is below sea level. You know, after taking two or three devastating hits, it perfected the art and science of flood control. America has one or two things to learn from the Dutch experience, without damaging the environment in the process.

## Were you able to salvage anything from your home?

This is a paper here, and you know what it means to get two pages of a sixty-page essay? What are you going to do with those two pages? Just smell it. I lost my computer. I lost all my records, vital documents, manuscripts, literary correspondence, and rare books. I had just returned from Nigeria, and I had my box full of rare books, books I was going to use for my teaching and research. I hadn't even opened the box before the storm came. It was by my bedside. Katrina took them all away. I'm not talking about clothes or whatever; those ones can be replaced. I particularly miss my literary correspondence, two or three files of them, including the latest exchanges between me and high school students in the UK who had one of my poems on their syllabus, and who kept sending me ask-the-author questions and comments to which I responded. I lost all those, and also my works-in-progress files. It's as if Katrina took away my memory. For months and months after the storm I couldn't sleep. Nor are my nights free of Katrina nightmares, even right up to this moment. Which is why I have found it so difficult so far to write about the experience. But I surely will. Eventually.

\* Antoine, Rebeca, "New Orleans is People," from *Voices Rising II: More Stories from the Katrina Narrative Project.* UNO Press, 2010, 363-380.

Born in Ikere-Ekiti, Western Nigeria, in 1947, NIYI OSUNDARE was educated at the University of Ibadan (BA Honours in English); University of Leeds (MA in Modern English); and York University, Toronto, (PhD in English). He is a playwright, essayist, and professor of English; has authored over fifteen books of poetry, two books of selected poems, four plays, two books of essays, and numerous scholarly articles and reviews. Among his many prizes are the Association of Nigerian Authors Poetry Prize, the Cadbury/ANA Poetry Prize (which he won on two occasions), the Commonwealth Poetry Prize, the Noma Award (Africa's most prestigious Book Award), the Tchicaya U Tam'si Award for African Poetry (generally regarded as "Africa's highest poetry prize"), and the Fonlon/Nichols Award for "excellence in literary creativity combined with significant contributions to Human Rights in Africa". In 2004, his award-winning book, *The Eye of the Earth*, was selected "One of Nigeria's Best 25 Books in the Past 25 Years" by Spectrum Books. He has been recipient of honorary doctorates from l'Universite de Toulouse-Le Mirail in France and Franklin Pierce University, Rindge, USA. A leading figure in the vanguard for the popularization of written poetry in Nigeria, he maintains a weekly poetry column in Nigeria's *Sunday Tribune*, a "Poem for the Month" column in *234NEXT*, and is a frequent contributor to the media on cultural and social matters. He is also a guest columnist for *Newswatch*, a prominent Nigerian newsmagazine, and an active contributor to public discourse on radio and television. A believer in poetry as performance, he has performed his works in many parts of the world, and his poetry has been translated into French, Italian, Slovenian, Czech, Spanish, Dutch, Arabic, and Korean. A fervent campaigner for Human Rights, social justice, and the environment, he was professor and former chair of English at the University of Ibadan in Nigeria, and he is currently Distinguished Professor of English at the University of New Orleans, USA, and constantly in touch with Nigeria, his social and cultural base.

# TITLES FROM BLACK WIDOW PRESS

## TRANSLATION SERIES

*Approximate Man and Other Writings*
by Tristan Tzara. Translated and edited
by Mary Ann Caws.

*Art Poétique* by Guillevic.
Translated by Maureen Smith.

*The Big Game*
by Benjamin Péret. Translated with an
introduction by Marilyn Kallet.

*Capital of Pain* by Paul Eluard.
Translated by Mary Ann Caws, Patricia
Terry, and Nancy Kline.

*Chanson Dada: Selected Poems* by Tristan
Tzara. Translated with an introduction and
essay by Lee Harwood.

*Essential Poems and Writings of Joyce
Mansour: A Bilingual Anthology*
Translated with an introduction by
Serge Gavronsky.

*Essential Poems and Prose of Jules Laforgue*
Translated and edited by Patricia Terry.

*Essential Poems and Writings of
Robert Desnos: A Bilingual Anthology*
Edited with an introduction and essay
by Mary Ann Caws.

*EyeSeas (Les Ziaux)* by Raymond Queneau.
Translated with an introduction by
Daniela Hurezanu and Stephen Kessler.

*Furor and Mystery & Other Writings*
by René Char. Edited and translated by
Mary Ann Caws and Nancy Kline.

*The Inventor of Love & Other Writings*
by Gherasim Luca. Translated by Julian
and Laura Semilian. Introduction by
Andrei Codrescu. Essay by Petre Răileanu.

*La Fontaine's Bawdy*
by Jean de la Fontaine. Translated with an
introduction by Norman R. Shapiro.

*Last Love Poems of Paul Eluard*
Translated with an introduction by
Marilyn Kallet.

*Love, Poetry (L'amour la poésie)*
by Paul Eluard. Translated with an essay
by Stuart Kendall.

*Poems of André Breton: A Bilingual
Anthology*
Translated with essays by Jean-Pierre
Cauvin and Mary Ann Caws.

*Poems of A.O. Barnabooth* by Valéry
Larbaud. Translated by Ron Padgett and
Bill Zavatsky.

*Preversities: A Jacques Prévert Sampler*
Translated and edited by Norman R.
Shapiro.

*The Sea and Other Poems* by Guillevic.
Translated by Patricia Terry. Introduction
by Monique Chefdor.

*To Speak, to Tell You?*
Poems by Sabine Sicaud. Translated by
Norman R. Shapiro. Introduction and
notes by Odile Ayral-Clause.

### forthcoming translations

*Essential Poems and Writings of Pierre Reverdy*
Edited by Mary Ann Caws. Translated by
Mary Ann Caws, Patricia Terry, Ron Padgett,
and John Ashbery.

*A Life of Poems, Poems of a Life* by Anna de
Noailles. Translated by Norman R. Shapiro.
Introduction by Catherine Perry.

# MODERN POETRY SERIES

*An Alchemist with One Eye on Fire*
by Clayton Eshleman

*Anticline* by Clayton Eshleman

*Archaic Design* by Clayton Eshleman

*Backscatter: New and Selected Poems*
by John Olson

*The Caveat Onus* by Dave Brinks
The complete cycle, four volumes in one.

*City Without People: The Katrina Poems*
by Niyi Osundare

*Concealments and Caprichos*
by Jerome Rothenberg

*Crusader-Woman* by Ruxandra Cesereanu
Translated by Adam J. Sorkin. Introduction by Andrei Codrescu.

*Curdled Skulls: Poems of Bernard Bador*
Translated by the author with Clayton
Eshleman.

*Endure: Poems by Bei Dao*
Translated by Clayton Eshleman and
Lucas Klein

*Fire Exit* by Robert Kelly

*Forgiven Submarine*
by Ruxandra Cesereanu and
Andrei Codrescu

*The Grindstone of Rapport:*
*A Clayton Eshleman Reader*
Forty years of poetry, prose, and
translations.

*Packing Light: New and Selected Poems*
by Marilyn Kallet

*The Present Tense of the World:*
*Poems 2000–2009*
by Amina Saïd. Translated with an
introduction by Marilyn Hacker.

*Signal from Draco: New and Selected Poems*
by Mebane Robertson

### forthcoming
### modern poetry titles

*Exile is My Trade: A Habib Tengour Reader*
Translated by Pierre Joris.

*from stone this running* by Heller Levinson

*Larynx Galaxy* by John Olson

*Memory Wing* by Bill Lavender

## LITERARY THEORY / BIOGRAPHY SERIES

*Revolution of the Mind:*
*The Life of André Breton*
by Mark Polizzotti. Revised
and augmented edition.

# WWW.BLACKWIDOWPRESS.COM